THE WORLD'S GREAT ACHIEVERS CELEBRATE OG MANDINO'S GREATEST ACHIEVEMENT!

"A terrific book! Its Commandments of Success are most inspirational and dynamic—a plan for peace of mind and a happy and successful life."

> —J. Willard Marriott, Chairman of the Board, Marriott Corporation

"Og Mandino has proven again to be a master storyteller, with the ability to identify principles that will enable all who choose to use them to achieve the true riches of life. This book is truly an act of love."

> —W. Clement Stone, Chairman and Founder, Combined International, Inc.

"I started reading *The Greatest Success in the World* and could not lay it down."

> —Richard M. Devos, President, Amway Corporation

Bantam Books by Og Mandino

OG MANDINO

THE GREATEST SUCCESS IN THE WORLD

BANTAM BOOKS
NEW YORK · TORONTO · LONDON · SYDNEY · AUCKLAND

THE GREATEST SUCCESS IN THE WORLD
A Bantam Book
PUBLISHING HISTORY
Bantam hardcover edition published September 1981
Bantam paperback edition / August 1982

ISBN 0-553-27825-8

Published simultaneously in the United States and Canada

Bantam Books are published by Bantam Books, a division of Bantam Doubleday Dell Publishing Group, Inc. Its trademark, consisting of the words "Bantam Books" and the portrayal of a rooster, is Registered in U.S. Patent and Trademark Office and in other countries. Marca Registrada. Bantam Books, 1540 Broadway, New York, New York 10036.

PRINTED IN THE UNITED STATES OF AMERICA

OPM   18   17   16   15

And behold, there was a man named Zacchaeus, which was the chief among the publicans, and he was rich.

And he sought to see Jesus who he was; and could not for the press, because he was little of stature.

Luke 19:2,3

It is a very plain and elementary truth, that the life, the fortune, and the happiness of every one of us, and, more or less, of those who are connected with us, do depend upon our knowing something of the rules of a game.

Thomas Huxley

Dedicated, with love, to my other father
and mother,
John and Rita Lang

THE GREATEST SUCCESS IN THE WORLD

CHAPTER 1

I must warn thee in advance.

The words you are about to read may put an end to your life.

It has been written that a useless life is far worse than an early death. If the years of your heartbeat, since you emerged from your mother's womb, have been poisoned by failure and frustration, heartbreak and discontent, defeat and self-pity, then I say unto you that you should terminate that miserable existence, immediately, and commence the rebuilding of a new life, a new being—one filled with love and pride and achievement and peace of mind.

Not only do I say that you should; I say that you *can*!

Not only do I say that you can; I say that you *will*—providing you accept and make use of the priceless legacy I am about to share with you.

My name is Joseph.

Would that I were an accomplished teller of tales, in full command of my proud language, instead of having spent a lifetime as a keeper of ledgers and accounts. Still, despite my many shortcomings, I must record what I know of Zacchaeus Ben Joshua for the benefit of untold generations to come so that they may be guided properly in their search for a better life. His story and, most important, his gift to mankind, must not vanish beneath the desert's unsympathetic sands along with the dried bones of those of us who knew and loved and learned so much from this special creature of God.

He was orphaned before the age of five.

Other children mocked his misshapen body—a huge head and wide shoulders set upon a round torso from which two spindly legs extended but refused to grow.

He had no schooling. Those precious years of youth had been spent in back-breaking labor, from sunrise to sunset, tilling the soil and picking the fruit on Herod's vast farms.

And yet, despite all his handicaps, he became the wealthiest man in all of Jericho, eventually acquiring title to more than half of all the irrigated farmland within a half-day's march of the city.

His home, surrounded by tall palms and date trees, exceeded in size and grandeur what had once been the winter palace of Herod and later, the despised king's weakling son.

An eminent scholar from Greece, having met him at the height of his career, returned to Athens and announced to his colleagues that he had finally met a man who had conquered the world and was not even aware of his accomplishments.

In his declining years he accepted a position that would have brought scorn and hate upon the head of any other, as it had to those who were his predecessors, but the love and respect of so many of the people, whose lives he had touched and changed for the better, never abated.

Near his end, he was involved in what I am certain was a miracle, although I had never, before, believed in miracles. No one who witnessed that mysterious event has ever been able to explain what they saw in any other terms—and it is the ingredients of this miracle that can and will change your life—as it has for so many others.

Pretend, if you will, that you are hearing my words rather than reading them.

Imagine that you are resting your weary head on my lap, as you may have done long ago, with your parents. This has been a day like all other days, when you have struggled with forces beyond your control to achieve a small allotment of peace and security for yourself and for those who love and depend on you.

Let me stroke away the bruises of this day's battles while I share, with you, the gold of one man's wisdom—wisdom that you can apply to how you think and feel and act so that you may be transformed, in time, from a dead and helpless leaf, buffeted by every breeze, into whatever proud manner of human being you desire to become.

Above all, exercise patience—and hear me out. We were brought together, you and I, for some purpose. Who can know God's plans for us? Who can explain the mystery of why you are reading these words at this particular moment in your life rather than the words of another?

Art thou prepared to step out of that old life and to begin anew?

At this point, is there not little to lose and everything to gain?

As his humble and self-appointed executor, allow me to transmit, to you, the most priceless asset from the estate of Zaccheus.

What you do with his unusual bequest ... is totally up to you.

CHAPTER 2

It has been said that memory is the only true treasure chest we possess and in it are stored all the jewels of our passing years. If that be so, then my most precious jewel, without question, is to have known and served the man whose name, in the language of our fathers, means "the just" or "the pure"—Zacchaeus.

Our first meeting was long ago, when we were young, in the crowded marketplace of Jericho where I had gone after being whipped by my stepfather for what I had resolved would be the last time. I was sitting on a stone bench, filled with self-pity and concern about my future, when I first saw Zacchaeus. Strapped to his back were several beams of cedar wood, and because of their great length and weight he was lunging from side to side in order to maintain his balance, greatly endangering the safety of passersby who heaped curses and threats upon him.

He was bent nearly double under that tremendous load, but as he passed I was shocked to hear him singing. What, I remember wondering, could this pitiful person have to sing about? Suddenly, before my eyes, he stumbled on the stones and fell beneath the heavy beams.

In my sorry mental state I had no desire to become involved with anyone else's misfortunes but when none who passed even so much as glanced at the still figure, I finally ran to him and began removing the giant wooden planks from above his body. His face was covered with blood. I knelt beside him and wiped at the deep gash in his forehead with the hem of my tunic. Eventually he began to stir, muttering words I could not understand. A kind woman from one of the nearby fruit stands brought a pitcher of water and a rag and the two of us washed his face until his eyelids fluttered and opened. Soon he was sitting up.

He grinned sheepishly at me and rubbed the top of his head while I stared in awe at the corded muscles of his massive biceps, rippling in the bright sun.

"They told me that I could not carry seven beams," he said ruefully.

"What?"

"The woodwork shop people," he replied. "They told me that no man, and certainly no one my size, could carry seven of these beams at one time, but I refused to believe them. How is one to know what one can accomplish unless one tries?"

Unsteadily he rose to his feet and I had all I could do to suppress my laughter. Dressed in appropriate costume he would have made a perfect clown in one of the many traveling circuses that pass through our city. He was all head and shoulders and arms and little else and his tunic hung to the pavement, completely concealing his lower appendages. In height he stood no taller than a boy of seven or eight, although he was certainly my age, sixteen, at least.

He came close to me, placed his two strong hands on my chest, looked up at me with large brown eyes filled with gratitude and said, in a deep, resonant voice, "Thank you, my friend, and God be with you."

I nodded and walked away. After twenty paces or so my curiosity made me look back, and when I did, I was unable to believe my eyes. There he was, piling the beams one upon another so that he could once again lift them to his shoulders! Fool! I ran back to him, for reasons I shall never understand, and said, "Stranger, you are not going to try the impossible again, are you?"

He dropped the seventh and last slab of wood noisily in place and stood, hands on hips, studying me for several moments. "Nothing is impossible," he said softly, "unless one agrees that it is."

I hesitated and then heard myself saying, "Let me help you. I have little to do. Take those straps and tie the beams together at both ends so that I can carry one end and you the other."

He opened his mouth as if to speak but said nothing. After the wood was bound tightly together, he lifted the front end and I struggled with the rear and we carried those monstrous beams, with many resting periods for me, to the very outskirts of the city where together we erected, on the road to Phasaelis, his very first roadside stall. From it, in the months to come, we sold only one crop—fat and juicy figs harvested by Zacchaeus and myself from a small plot of land he had purchased after five hard years of toil.

For the next half-century, and more, we were never far from each other's side—always prepared to lighten the other's load whenever assistance was needed. True friends are never acquired by chance; they are always gifts from God.

CHAPTER 3

Surrounded on all sides by lifeless desert and desolate hills of gray stone, Jericho is a green paradise of fertile plains fed by many springs and aqueducts. So prized are its crops that at one time Mark Antony presented all its balsam plantations and surrounding land to Cleopatra as an imperial gift. In time the seductive queen sold them to Herod who derived great revenue from the fruits of his purchase until his death.

When Herod's son, Archelaus, was removed from power by Rome, Jericho and all of Judaea was placed under the rule of Roman procurators. These men, usually with a military background, cared little for farming, only for the taxes that might be derived from each crop and so, year after year, Zacchaeus acquired more and more royal land to add to his first small grove of fig trees. As the keeper of his books, I can remember times when more than two thousand farmhands were in his employ, not to mention the three hundred or so necessary to service the produce stalls that we erected both outside and inside the city's walls.

As the enterprises of Zacchaeus flourished, his faith and trust in my ability and judgment increased until we eventually became closer than are most brothers. His first storehouse for cotton was built here, in Jericho, on my advice. In time it was replaced by a great palace, with a connecting warehouse, extending for more than twelve hundred cubits with no equal in size, even in Jerusalem.

My recollections of those other days are as vivid, in my mind, as this morning's sunrise. In a steady parade, caravans would arrive at our loading docks from the merchants of the world, either purchasing our many crops with gold and silver or bartering with their own exotic and much-desired products from strange lands. Oil, wine, and pottery arrived often from Marcus Filicius of Rome. From Crespi, of Sicily, came exotic jewelry and sturdy livestock. Malthus, of Ethiopia, shipped tortoiseshells and pungent spices for the wealthy women of Jericho while Lino, from far-off Spain, always sent objects of gold and bars of iron. The Germans provided furs and polished amber; carpets and rare perfumes, and leathers were uncrated from Dion of Persia, and Wo Sang Pi sent lustrous bolts of silk from distant Shanghai.

In return, the caravans departed with crates of fruit from the nubk-tree, bags of dates, bales of cotton, honey, flasks of zukkum oil, bananas, henna dye, sugarcane, grapes, maize, figs, and the most highly prized balsam oil—all grown on the ever-increasing lands of Zacchaeus whose warehouses eventually became stores from which the entire civilized world was served.

To the people of Jericho, Zacchaeus was always

looked upon with far greater respect than most princes of commerce, plying their wares. For the poor and the suffering of Jericho, both young and old, condemned in most cases to a life of misery and futility by circumstances beyond their control, my master became their candle of hope, their deliverer from discomfort, rescuer from starvation, healer of disease, and shelterer from life's most grinding adversities.

Beginning with our second year together, when his farms were still few and small, I was enjoined by Zacchaeus, as his trusted bookkeeper, to distribute an unprecedented proportion of half of all our profits to the needy. As our business increased, more and more of the city's poor were fed and clothed; buildings were erected to shelter the aged and the orphaned; doctors were imported from Egypt and Rome to tend to the crippled and diseased; and teachers were recruited to instruct the young. Even the lowliest of beggars and derelicts were removed from the gutters and cared for until some semblance of their dignity was returned to them. It is impossible, even for one as proficient at figures as me, to calculate how much gold and silver was expended, or how many lives were salvaged, through the master's unflinching generosity.

Unlike most of the wealthy, who allowed their great deeds of charity to be proclaimed throughout the land, it was in keeping with the character of Zacchaeus that his benevolent acts were always performed with no fanfare and great modesty. Even when that renowned scholar from Athens, after learning of all that Zacchaeus had accomplished in less than thirty years, exclaimed that he was undoubtedly "the greatest success in the world," I remember Zacchaeus blushing and shrugging his huge shoulders. His response to such praise was always the same. He had been blessed with far more material goods than any single human deserved, and he was only lending a small helping hand to God in partial repayment for all that God had bestowed on him.

Zacchaeus ruled over his kingdom, as he laughingly called his conglomeration of farms, with a fair but firm hand. Only one tragedy marred those first decades of prosperity and it ultimately brought us closer together, if such could be possible.

How strange it is that grief knits two hearts into a stronger bond than happiness ever can.

CHAPTER 4

During the days, Zacchaeus and I saw very little of each other as his farming empire grew. I was usually in one of our warehouses taking inventory, supervising a shipment, or monitoring the keeping of our many accounts. He, on the other hand, was always traveling from farm to farm to assist our stewards in resolving their many problems, and very often actually toiling in the fields with the laborers. He was a fortunate man. He loved his work.

In the evenings, since neither of us were wed, we always dined together, taking advantage of those restful hours to discuss the progress of our operations and to plan for the future.

I shall never forget one night when the master was strangely silent while he nibbled at his food, responding to my remarks with only an occasional nod. This unusual behavior continued throughout our meal until I could endure such treatment no longer.

"Zacchaeus, what is wrong?"

He raised his head and stared blankly in my direction but did not speak.

"A serious situation on one of the farms?" I persevered. "Where were you today?"

"To the north," he replied softly.

"And how are Reuben's cotton and Jonathan's sugarcane enduring their smaller allotment of water?"

"Very well, very well. They both expect to exceed last year's record crops."

Then there was silence again. I had never known him to act in such a manner toward me before.

"Are you ill?" I finally asked.

He shook his head. More silence. I am a stubborn man. I decided to wait him out. We would sit at the table until tomorrow's sunrise, so far as I was concerned, until he finally confided in me.

My wait was not long. With an agonizing moan, Zacchaeus suddenly leaped from his couch and stood before me, raising his linen tunic to bare his thin childlike legs.

"Look at me, Joseph!" he cried. "Look at this terrible excuse for the body of a man! Consider this head, large enough for two people and already growing bald. See these shoulders and arms and this strange round chest and then look—look—at the miserable thin reeds that must support all this ugliness. I am truly a joke against the human race, locked within this terrible cage of a twisted body from which there is no escape until death. A prisoner forever, in a prison with no doors! Why did God treat me in this way, Joseph?"

He slumped back on the couch and buried his head in his hands, sobbing. I was too shocked to speak. In all our years together, the subject of his short, strangely formed body had only arisen twice and both times after we had consumed more than our share of dinner wine. On those two rare occasions, as I can recall, our conversations had commenced with my suggesting that it was time that he take upon himself a wife to share his good fortune and both times he had smiled sadly and said that no woman in her right mind would allow herself to be betrothed to only half a man, and an ugly one at that.

Betrothed?

I reached out and touched his shoulder gently. "Zacchaeus, did you spend much time with old Jonathan today?"

He peered at me warily, through spread fingers. "We were together for most of the morning. Why?"

"And how is his lovely daughter, Leah? I imagine she must be growing more beautiful with each passing season."

Those magnificent shoulders sagged and Zacchaeus looked away. "Joseph, we have been together so long, you and I, that even what is in the heart of one is little more than an open scroll to the other. I would trade all my farms to have Leah as my wife," he sighed.

"And how does she feel?"

"How is one to know, for a certainty? She is always kind to me, and pleasant, when I visit her father, but after all isn't she expected to act that way toward the homely little rich man who owns the land which supports her and her family? And what if I had the courage to ask her parents for permission to discuss marriage with her and she agreed to my proposal? Would she not be marrying me solely for the security and the good things I am able to provide for her? How could she ever feel any love for the man in this ... this cage?" he grimaced, rubbing his hands from his head to his toes.

"Zacchaeus," I said, rising: "I have never told you an untruth in the years we have labored together."

"I know."

"Listen to me, I beg you. Many years ago, when I first saw you in the marketplace, I took pity on you. That pity lasted only a short time before I came to realize that you were more a man than I would ever be. Gradually, as I watched you accomplish great wonders, piling success upon success, you became to me a giant, perfect in form and figure. I still see you that way, blinded if you will, by your many talents, your courage, your intelligence, your compassion for others, and your great strength—not in your arms but in your soul. Zacchaeus, I would wager my life that Leah sees you exactly as I do."

They were wed within the year. Four years later they moved into a palace, built for her by Zacchaeus. Another twelve months passed and just when the two had become resigned to never being blessed with any offspring, Leah announced that she was with child.

Of course, Zacchaeus was positive that his first-born would be a son. Month after month, whenever we were together, it always required great effort on my part to bring our conversation around to business. Already, the future father was making grandiose plans for his heir. The lad would have the finest stable of Arabian stallions, teachers would be brought from Rome and Corinth and Jerusalem to instruct him properly, a special room in the palace would contain nothing but toys, and some-day his son would be the largest landowner in all of Judaea, with servants always at his disposal and the most powerful men in the world as his friends.

"Look at this, Joseph," he said to me one morning, opening a small box of polished walnut and removing, from its silk lining, a delicately carved piece of ivory, smaller than my fist. Over the years I had become so expert in works of art produced from elephant tusks that I could even detect whether they had come from the tusks of an African or a Chinese elephant by their color and texture. This was undoubtedly a Chinese piece, carved to the finest of detail into what looked like a small bird cage. Inside, a tiny bird, also of ivory, rolled back and forth on the floor of the cage.

"This must have taken months to complete," I gasped. "Do you realize that the entire piece was fashioned from a single piece of solid tusk and done so expertly that the small bird inside was carved from its center without harming the count-less thin bars of white that enclose it? I have never seen anything quite like it! It is worth a fortune!"

"I have great compassion for that little bird," he smiled sadly, rubbing the small white cage gently against his cheek. "As you can see, there are no doors to his prison either."

"Where did you get such a treasure?"

"It is a gift from our caravan friend, Wo Sang Pi, for my future son."

"For your son?" I asked, puzzled.

"Yes, for my son. It is a rattle, Joseph—a rattle to amuse my baby on those rare occasions when I cannot be in the palace to play with him."

Tears flow down my cheeks, even as I write this, for that rattle was never grasped by tiny fingers, nor did any of the dreams and plans of Zacchaeus for his son ever come to pass. The infant, a boy, was delivered stillborn and the mother, beautiful, frail Leah, failed to survive the delivery.

The following twelve months were an agonizing period for all of us who were close to Zacchaeus. He retired to his huge bedroom and severed himself from all contact with the outside world, including me. Only Shemer, the first servant hired by Leah upon their move into the palace, was allowed to bring him food and fresh clothing and whenever we inquired as to our master's condition the old man would shake his head and walk away.

One day, as I was straining over my ledgers and accounts, I felt a hard and familiar hand on my shoulder. "Greetings, bookkeeper," Zacchaeus said calmly, looking and sounding just as I had remembered him before the tragedy.

"Greetings to you, Master! Welcome back."

He nodded toward the open ledger. "Are we still profitable?"

"More than ever."

"Merely proof of what I have been saying for years, Joseph. You are as valuable to this enterprise as I am, if not more so."

"I appreciate your kind words, Zacchaeus," I replied, "but they are only spoken out of your great generosity. Beginning with that first roadside stall, all of this was built because of your vision and perseverance. I was, and I am, only a useful tool for you and I am honored to be that. All great achievers, such as yourself, need others like me to carry out their instructions."

He patted my head. "Joseph, I have a favor to ask of you. How many children would you estimate are living in this city who have not yet reached their tenth birthday?"

My mouth, I am certain, flew open. "How m-m-many children . . . tenth birthday?"

"Yes."

I must confess that for a brief moment I did consider the possibility that Zacchaeus' tragic loss and his long months of seclusion had affected his mind. Finally I replied, "Perhaps two thousand or so."

"Very good. I want you to have signs posted, throughout the city, inviting all of them and their parents to a party in our courtyard, four days from now, on the seventh day of Nisan."

Bookkeepers cannot survive unless they are competent in the memorizing of dates. "The seventh day of Nisan," I stumbled over my words, "is that not the day, a year ago, that . . . that . . . ?"

". . . that I lost my family, my Leah and my son? You are accurate, as always, my dear friend." There was no sadness or self-pity in his warm voice. "Joseph, we shall have a birthday party, on the day of my son's birth, not only to honor him but every child of Jericho, most of whom have never been recognized on any anniversary of their arrival into this world. Withdraw whatever amount you need from our treasury and make all necessary arrangements so that everyone will be royally feasted and be certain that each child receives a plaything that will be his or her very own."

"Two thousand! That will require a fortune," I gasped.

"It should cause us but little concern. And think what it will mean to each of them."

And so it came to pass that on the seventh day of Nisan, the spacious marble courtyard outside the palace of Zacchaeus became a playground filled with children, laughing and running and crying out with joy while they gorged themselves on delectables that many had never seen or tasted before. And no one enjoyed the festivities more than Zacchaeus. He laughed at the hired clowns, assisted the young into donkey carts, tossed multicolored balls at the feet of dancing children, and exhorted timid parents to become involved in games with their young. Eventually, flushed of face and short of breath, he took his seat by my side and watched, constantly applauding the happiness that paraded before our eyes.

Late in the day, after the crowd had grown smaller, a young boy, fingers in mouth, raced close to where we were sitting. Zacchaeus reached out his hands and the lad leaped boldly into his host's lap.

"And what are you called, my son?" Zacchaeus asked.

"Nathaniel."

A small cry escaped from the lips of Zacchaeus. He recovered his composure and said, "That is a good name. If I had a son he would be `called Nathaniel."

The small boy giggled and snuggled closer, chewing noisily on his moist stalk of sugarcane.

"Tell me, Nathaniel," Zacchaeus said, holding the youth aloft so that he was looking directly into his large brown eyes, "if you could have any wish granted, today, what would you desire?"

The giggling ceased and the youth frowned in contemplation, wiping at his dirt-streaked face as he looked around. Then he pointed toward the palace, behind us.

"You would like that big place?" Zacchaeus chuckled. "But if I gave it to you, where would I live?"

The boy shook his head impatiently. "No, no . . . the white . . . the white. . . ."

"The white walls?" asked Zacchaeus, turning to me for assistance I was unable to render.

Nathaniel pointed to the painted walls of the palace again. Then he turned, in Zacchaeus' arms, and pointed through two palm trees toward the nearby walls of the city. "Dirty walls . . . dirty walls."

"Ah ha!" roared Zacchaeus. "Now I understand. You would like to see the city's walls as white and clean as those of my house!"

The youth nodded excitedly.

Zacchaeus winced and turned in time to catch me struggling very hard to keep from laughing. It was one of the few times I had ever seen the master flustered. "Sire, you must understand," I chuckled, "that wishes are one of the few pleasures of the poor yet they have no comprehension of what is required to transform their desires into reality."

He shook his head. "Joseph, wishing is the first step toward accomplishment. If a person does not first wish, then he or she will never make plans to achieve anything."

Zacchaeus lowered Nathaniel to the courtyard floor, clasped the youth's head close to his breast, and kissed him on the forehead.

"Thy will be done, Nathaniel. In your honor and in honor of all the children of Jericho, the walls will be painted white."

And so they were. Within a few weeks after seeking and receiving approval from both the shocked elders of the city and the Roman centurion, headquartered in Jericho, the grimy terra-cotta walls encircling the city were whitewashed, on both sides and even on top, by more than five hundred laborers.

Every year thereafter, the young of Jericho were treated to a party in the courtyard on the seventh day of Nisan and the city's walls received fresh coats of white at the master's expense.

Inasmuch as I had never been blessed with a family of my own, I finally accepted his kind invitation to move into the palace with him and the two of us grew old together, becoming more and more alike with each passing year, just as two pines on the mountaintop, exposed to the same winds and rains, eventually become little more than mirrors of each other.

And our enterprises continued to multiply and flourish in peace and tranquillity until, one day, we received a surprise visit from the newly appointed Roman procurator of Judaea.

CHAPTER 5

Pontius Pilate was short in stature but he carried himself with an air that demanded respect for his rank. With his dark skin and closely cropped silver hair he was the epitome of every Roman officer from his polished breastplate to his silver-studded boots. Heavy perspiration on his face and neck were the only blemishes to his impressive image of power as he strutted through our courtyard, hands clasped behind his back, carrying on a steady conversation with Zacchaeus in Greek, our language in common, while the city's chief officer, centurion Marcus Crispus, and I, marched silently behind.

Upon completing our tour of the palace and the warehouse, we rested in the shade of the atrium and Shemer produced silver goblets into which he poured cool white wine.

Pilate was the first to raise his goblet. "I salute you, Zacchaeus. From what you have been kind enough to show me, I can understand why many call you the richest man in Jericho. An almost unbelievable achievement in a single lifetime. How old are you, sir?"

Zacchaeus sipped lightly on the wine and smiled. "I am well into the evening of my years, procurator, but there is still a child in my heart. I am afraid that, like all others, my desire is to live a long life without the necessity of growing old. On my next birthday I shall have counted sixty-seven very precious years."

Pilate shook his head in admiration. "You are an amazing man, Zacchaeus. Your deeds must certainly equal those of that famous merchant from Damascus, he who is known as the greatest salesman in the world."*

"I have known Hafid for many years. His countless trade caravans load and unload at our warehouse many times during the year."

"This palace of yours is magnificent and your warehouse certainly has no equal, even in Rome."

Zacchaeus shrugged his wide shoulders. "My wealth is not here, sir. It is out there, on the farms, growing on fig and date trees and on cotton plants and sugarcanes, and even there it would be worthless without my greatest asset—the loyal people who tend the plants and trees with love and concern. I would be most proud to show you my treasures providing you can spend two or three days here with us."

Pilate raised both hands. "That will not be necessary. My predecessor, Valerius Gratus, took great pains to supply me with a complete report on all that you have accomplished here. And Rome is

*The Greatest Salesman in the World, by Og Mandino; hardcover edition published by Frederick Fell Publishers, Inc., 1968, paperback edition published by Bantam Books, Inc., 1974.

most grateful for your large tax remittances that have contributed so much to our maintenance of peace throughout the empire. Tell me, since you live here in Jericho, is it required that you also pay taxes to the Temple in Jerusalem?"

"Of course. Caesar receives what is due him but so does God."

I saw Pilate's jaw tighten and listened with a mounting premonition of danger as these two strong men continued to exchange words. Why was the new procurator here? Procurators rarely made social calls, especially in Judaea, preferring to remain in the governor's sumptuous residence at Caesarea except for our holy days when they would appear in Jerusalem, with additional troops, to prevent the large gathering of worshipers from getting out of hand.

Zacchaeus seemed to read my mind. "We are most honored by your visit, sir. In all the years that Gratus ruled as governor of Judaea, his presence never once graced our home."

Pilate ignored the master's unspoken question and pointed to a small section of the city's wall that could be seen through a grove of palm trees. "Were not the walls of this city leveled by what your people claimed was a miracle, many years ago?"

"Not these walls," corrected Zacchaeus, "but those of the old city that stood directly to the north of the present one. After our people had escaped from the bondage of Egypt, more than fourteen centuries ago, they wandered for many years before crossing the Jordan and arriving on these green plains in their search for a homeland. However, the people of Jericho rejected them and locked the gates of their city but God instructed our leader, Joshua, as to how to proceed against the enemy within."

"A plan of battle—from your God?" Pilate made no attempt to hide the scorn in his voice.

"It could be called that. Each day our people, obeying God's orders, marched completely around the city's wall behind seven priests blowing on ram's horns. Following the march they would retire to their nearby camp. Then, on the seventh day, our forces marched around the wall a total of seven times and at the end of the seventh encirclement they all turned and faced toward the city. When the priests blew on their trumpets again, the multitude raised their arms and shouted and the stones shook and cracked until the mighty walls tumbled to the ground whereupon the city was captured and burned to ashes. You can still see its ruins, only a short march from here. Most of this wall around the new city was built by Herod in his early days as king."

"Very interesting," Pilate said, waving his goblet as a signal for Shemer to refill it. "And I understand that the bright coating of white, now covering the wall, is your doing. I applaud such civic pride, Zacchaeus. It is a most pleasant sight, as one rides down through the desolate landscape from Jerusalem, to see this shining circle of white stone surrounded by the greenery of what must be, for the most part, farms of yours. Jerusalem should have such a generous benefactor."

Zacchaeus frowned. "Jerusalem needs no such ornamentation. The Temple is there and God is there. That is sufficient."

Pilate's eyes narrowed. "The Roman fortress, Antonia, is also there."

Zacchaeus smiled and nodded. "Who can forget?"

I held my breath. The course of the conversation was not a healthy one. At last the procurator placed his goblet noisily on the table and turned to his silent subordinate, Marcus Crispus. "Centurion," he said curtly, "perhaps you should inform our host as to the purpose of our visit."

Marcus was a kind and gentle man. Through the years we had dealt with him often and had always been treated fairly. He leaned toward Zacchaeus and I could see the fear of Pilate in his eyes. His voice was little more than a whisper.

"Sir, you are well acquainted with the chief tax collector here?"

"Samuel? Who could not be familiar with the chief among the publicans, especially since he regularly removes, from my treasury, so much of my gold and silver. Yes, I know him well. We have been friends for many years despite my low opinion of his occupation and the anguish he causes me and my bookkeeper."

Marcus forced a smile. "Samuel is exceedingly ill and he has asked to be relieved of his responsibility as the overseer of all tax collectors in this district."

Zacchaeus clasped his hands together. "That is sad news. He is a good man, a good husband and father, and he worships his God faithfully despite the hatred he is forced to endure as a publican. He was also an honest man in all our dealings and honest tax collectors are as rare as a miracle. I shall miss him. Has the honored procurator selected his replacement, as yet?"

Before Marcus could reply, Pilate rose impatiently and placed his hand on Zacchaeus' shoulder. "Sir, I have chosen you to assume Samuel's position as the chief publican of Rome in this city!"

Zacchaeus' head snapped back as if he had been struck. All that I can remember of those next few moments are the heavy poundings in my chest. The master's face had turned gray and he stared up at Pilate, shaking his head violently from side to side.

"You cannot be serious, sir. I would never engage in such a repugnant undertaking against my own people, even if I were starving. Why do you come to me with such a suggestion when there are many who would lick your boots for such an opportunity to fill their purse. Why me, of all people?"

Pilate calmly settled back into his chair and held up his right hand, fingers spread wide apart. "For many reasons, Zacchaeus. First," he said, touching his thumb, "you are an honest man. Second," he continued, wiggling his little finger, "you are wise in the ways of business and money. None of the sixty or so publicans, in their tollbooths or in the city, would dare withhold any of their collections from you. Next, you are already wealthy and so money would be of little enticement to you. . . ."

Zacchaeus, in a rare act for him, interrupted the procurator. Lowering his voice as if he were carefully explaining some fact of life to a child, he said, "Perhaps you do not understand, sir, since you have only recently arrived in Judaea, but among our people there is no more repugnant way for a person to earn his living than to be a gatherer of taxes from his own people, for delivery to Caesar. Only a harlot or a herdsman is held in lower repute and it is said, in our faith, that repentance for tax gatherers in the eyes of God is almost impossible. Why should I sacrifice the respect of every citizen in Jericho and jeopardize my relationship with God by taking upon myself, at my old age, a calling I detest and never could perform with a clear conscience? With all due respect, sir, I suggest you seek your chief publican elsewhere."

With that, the master rose as if to signal that the discussion was terminated but the procurator remained seated, a tight smile on his lips.

"Zacchaeus, I have found my publican. I know of your countless charities and the wonders you have wrought for this city. You are, without doubt, the most beloved person in Jericho and from your actions, through the years, it is obvious that you have great love and compassion for all your fellow-citizens."

Pilate paused as if he were choosing his words carefully. "Now I ask you—would you, or your God, prefer that I select, as chief publican, someone else who may turn out to be the sort that would condone the robbery and extortion that we all know exists in the collecting of taxes? You must be aware of the countless ways in which one's life can be made almost unbearable by insolent and thieving publicans despite all our efforts to police their activities. Are you not willing to give a little more of yourself to see that so many lives are made no more unbearable than they already are? Or, are you one of those who find it easy to give only when there is little sacrifice or personal discomfort involved?"

Thus it was that the most unlikely man for the position, in all of Jericho, became the city's chief tax collector. Eventually the citizenry recovered from their initial shock, and after Zacchaeus turned over the daily management of all his enterprises to me, he threw himself as zealously into his new challenge as he always had done to every undertaking.

Dishonest and rapacious toll road collectors were dismissed as soon as they were detected; equitable rates of taxation were levied on all farms and places of business and, through constant inspection, Zacchaeus made certain that few, if any, were ever cheated or mistreated by any publican under his supervision.

Zacchaeus served in his distasteful position of authority for more than four years, years that took a great toll on his spirit. Gradually he began to brood about the condition of his life, even mentioning death on several occasions as if joining his beloved Leah, in her marble tomb behind the palace, would be a comforting and welcome relief.

Who could have foreseen that, one day, my seventy-one-year-old beloved master would climb a common sycamore tree, or that the consequences of this seemingly ludicrous act would completely change the remainder of his life?

CHAPTER 6

Herod's deserted palace in Jericho had long ago been taken over by Rome for use in a variety of government functions. In one of its former large dining halls, whose closed doors were always guarded by a somber legionary, Marcus Crispus had established his military headquarters from where he kept a watchful eye on the activities of the city with the help of a small contingent of soldiers supplied by Pontius Pilate.

Here, also, were located the offices of the chief publican, staffed by at least a dozen clerks who received the daily collections from the tax collectors in the area, counted the money, and prepared it for weekly shipment to the treasury of Pilate at the fortress in Jerusalem. From there the money was transported under guard to Vitellius, the legate headquartered in Antioch, who consolidated all receipts from the provinces and shipped them to Rome.

Since I had just visited with the manager of one of our larger fruit stalls, close by the palace, I decided to pay Zacchaeus a surprise visit. The door to his office was closed and just as I proceeded to knock, I heard angry voices shouting inside. With unusual discretion, for me, I backed away from the door and sat at a nearby bench to wait. After only a short while, the door was flung open and a tall figure rushed by me so swiftly that I saw only the back of his gray tunic and his bowed head as his fleeting sandals echoed noisily on the marble tiles.

"Thief! Robber! Never, never let me see your face again!"

Zacchaeus was standing in the office doorway, shaking his huge fist at the retreating man. He grinned when he saw me and beckoned with his head for me to enter, closing the door behind us.

"Trouble?" I asked, after we were seated.

"Always from the same group," he sighed. "Those who collect road tolls are constant thorns in my flesh. They prey even on the pilgrims traveling up to Jerusalem for the holy days, humiliating them by insisting that every bag containing their possessions be opened for inspection and even extorting extra duties for the gifts these poor people are bringing to the Temple for Passover. This is the worst time of year. I would need a thousand pairs of eyes to watch over all my greedy publicans. That one who just flew by you had imposed such a heavy road tax on one family that they were unable to pay. Do you know what he did? He finally allowed them to pass only after they agreed to exchange their healthy ass for an old and sick one belonging to him! Fortunately, they had the courage to report his crime to me and when they return here, this afternoon, they will receive full restitution."

He held up a small purse which I assumed, from its heft, was filled with coins. "Joseph," He cried, closing his eyes, "what am I doing here when I could be enjoying the little time remaining to me in my beautiful fields of green, under the blue sky, breathing the aroma of the balsam and the date?"

"You are here, Zacchaeus, to protect those who are powerless to protect themselves. Have you not reminded me of that on countless occasions during these past few years?"

He shook his head and sighed. "Am I my brother's keeper?"

"You have always been, Zacchaeus, and you will never change."

He scowled and hastily turned to another subject. "Tell me about our farms. Has that aqueduct to the west been swept clean?"

Before I could reply there was a loud pounding on the door.

"Enter!" Zacchaeus roared.

The door burst open to reveal a young man, clad only in loincloth, his well-muscled chest heaving violently, while moans of one gasping for air came from his open mouth.

Zacchaeus leaped up and ran to the youth. "What is wrong, Aaron? Has something happened to your father?"

The master turned toward me. "His father is a toll collector on the road from Perea. A good man."

Zacchaeus led the youth toward a bench, handed him a flask of water, and stroked his neck comfortingly for several moments. "Now tell me, son, what brings you here in such a state?"

"My father told me to report to you as swiftly as I could."

"Report? Report what? Has he been robbed in his booth? Has harm come to him?"

"No, no, my father is well and sends you his greetings. But he wanted you to know that he was just witness to a miracle. A blind man, who sits each day near the booth begging alms from those who pass, has just had his sight restored by that prophet from Galilee, the one called Jesus."

"He saw this with his own eyes?"

"He did. It occurred only a few paces from his booth."

"How did it happen? Did he tell you?"

The youth nodded and inhaled deeply. "He said that Jesus and his followers had already passed through the tollgate when the blind man called after him saying, 'Son of David, have mercy on me.'"

Zacchaeus paled. "He said 'Son of David'?"

"Yes. And when Jesus heard that, he turned and walked back to where the blind man was sitting and asked what it was that he could do for him, and the man asked that he might receive his sight and Jesus replied, 'Receive thy sight: thy faith hath saved thee.'"

"And then what?" Zacchaeus asked, anxiously leaning forward.

The young man shrugged and smiled. "The blind man leaped to his feet and cried out to all who were present that he could see and when Jesus and the others continued down the road he hurried to join them."

Zacchaeus stared down at his hands until I broke the silence. "Who is this Jesus, Master?"

"Have ye not heard, Joseph? He is the young man from Nazareth who raised one called Lazarus from the dead, in nearby Bethany, only a few months ago."

"A magician?"

Zacchaeus looked at me strangely. "No, I do not think so. Where is he now, Aaron?"

"He and his followers, along with the blind man who received his sight, are coming this way. They are on the Jericho road. I passed them as I raced to bring you the news. They should arrive here, in the city, within the hour."

"Thank you, Aaron—and thank your father. Tell him that I said he has a fine son."

After the youth had departed, Zacchaeus began pacing the floor, hands behind his back, head bowed. I remained silent from past experience, having observed him act in such a manner many hundreds of times through the years, usually when he was trying to resolve a difficult problem that had arisen within our business. He had always claimed that he could think more clearly when walking or performing some physical task rather than sitting on his posterior. Now there was an old familiar spring to his step, one I had not seen for many years. Even his eyes sparkled and his face seemed to have shed many of its recently acquired dark lines.

"Why are you staring at me so, Joseph?"

"I-I-I don't know, sir. I don't know except that you look different to me, somehow."

"Do you have any special plans for this afternoon?"

"There are three more of our stalls, nearby, that I should inspect."

He brushed my words aside with a wave of his hand. "Visit them tomorrow. Let us go, you and I, out to the street and find ourselves a shady spot under a tree where we shall wait until this Jesus passes. I would like to see the kind of man who can make the blind see and the dead return to life."

"Man? Zacchaeus, a man cannot perform such acts. Either he is a trickster, who uses accomplices to fool the people or . . . or . . ."

The master stood still, waiting for me to finish the sentence. I could not.

"Come, Joseph," he smiled. "Let us be our own witnesses."

CHAPTER 7

The great caravan roads from Syria, to the north, and Arabia, to the east, meet and join on the eastern outskirts of Jericho before cutting through the heart of the city as a wide stone road, paved expertly by the Romans. At the western border, the city's main street once again becomes dirt before it commences its tortuous climb to the city of Jerusalem, at least six hours away by foot.

When Zacchaeus and I arrived at the main thoroughfare it was choked with humanity. Long trade caravans, always a common sight as they traveled along the busy highway, had been joined by huge throngs of pilgrims from Perea and Galilee on their way up to the Holy City for Passover. And now, for the first time in my memory, there were crowds lining the pavement on both sides, all looking toward the east expectantly.

Zacchaeus paused near a man and woman. In the woman's arms a young girl lay sleeping. "For what reason are ye waiting here?" he asked.

The woman clutched her child closer to her bosom and stepped back from Zacchaeus, whom she obviously recognized, but the man answered him immediately. "We are waiting to see the miracle-worker, sir, a man called Jesus from Nazareth. They tell us that he is certain to pass this way soon on his journey up to Jerusalem for Passover. Our daughter has been crippled since birth. She cannot even stand by herself. Perhaps Jesus will bless her and make her whole if we are fortunate enough to catch his attention. But there are so many. . . ."

Zacchaeus reached inside his tunic and placed something in the young mother's hand. "For the little one," he said, patting the woman's arm. I did not need to ask what he had done. One of my duties was to keep the small pouch he carried on his person always filled with gold coins.

The crowd was at least three deep along the road for as far as we could see in both directions, and so there was little sense in walking farther in the stifling heat. We halted beneath an old sycamore tree whose gnarled branches reached far out over the road and also provided welcome shade for us as we mingled with the noisy gathering who were beginning, in their impatience, to shout taunts and insults at every rural pilgrim family who passed by on their way to Jerusalem.

"Why do they do that?" sighed Zacchaeus, shaking his head angrily. "Why do we continue to breed little minds who can find no recompense for their own failures other than to belittle and mock the talents, even the dress, of others? When will everyone realize that we are all equal in the eyes of God?"

"A mob has no mind of its own, Zacchaeus. They are capable of committing vile acts, collectively, that as individuals they would never dare attempt."

"Yes, I know. I wonder how they will treat Jesus?"

Down the road, to the east, we soon heard shouts that gradually grew into loud cheering. The crowd near us began to surge slowly into the street. A woman nearby, tugging at the hands of a young boy, began screaming as the words, "He's coming, he's coming!" spread rapidly along the road. I raised myself up on my toes in order to have a clearer view, now caught up in the fervor of the throng over a man I had never even known existed until this morning.

Zacchaeus began tugging at my tunic. "Can you see him, Joseph? Has he appeared yet?"

The master, because of his lack of height, could see little but the backs of those who stood in front of him, and yet I knew that he would never take advantage of his authority to force himself to the front ranks. All I could do was to try to act as his eyes.

"Yes, yes," I shouted above the clamor. "Now I can see him! He is perhaps a hundred paces away, walking at the head of a large group and smiling and waving at the people."

"What does he look like? Tell me, please!"

"Tall—taller than most of the others. Hair is dark brown, hanging loosely to his shoulders. He has a beard. Walks with head held high. He is wearing a white tunic and over his shoulders, even in this heat, he has a red robe. Now he is perhaps fifty paces away. A young girl—she has just run out of the crowd and handed him a flower. Now a woman is holding her child above her head and crying out to him. He keeps waving and smiling but continues walking without pause and . . ."

I turned and looked down. The tugging on my tunic had ceased and Zacchaeus was nowhere in sight! Two men were pointing up and laughing. I looked up—and saw Zacchaeus! He was climbing our shady sycamore tree, inching up higher and higher and moving out on the lowest heavy branch until his body was directly over the approaching party. I was too shocked to cry out to him and, I must confess, more than a little embarrassed at such a foolish act by a man of his age and position. I shifted my attention back to Jesus just as he passed in front of me. He looked younger than I had expected and as he turned in my direction I could see that his face and neck were scorched from the sun and his eyes were inflamed.

Jesus passed under the low branch of the sycamore tree and continued forward for ten or more paces before he halted, turned, and looked up, blinking at the uncommon sight of an old man swaying precariously in a tree. The crowd grew silent. Jesus pointed up at the figure above his head and said, in a voice that all could hear, "Zacchaeus, make haste, and come down; for today I must abide at thy house."

There was a great lump in my throat as I watched, through uncontrollable tears, as my master, having climbed down from his perch, limped out into the street with his tiny legs and reached up with open arms to embrace the young preacher.

Of course there were those who wondered why Jesus had chosen to rest in the house of a publican, a sinner some murmured among themselves, and others were mystified, including myself, as to how Jesus knew his name. Most of the people, however, cheered as Zacchaeus and Jesus walked off together, after the master had introduced him to me, while the young man's followers dispersed to houses of friends.

To my everlasting regret I was unable to spend any time with the two of them. A messenger was waiting for me when I returned to the palace, informing me that the caravan of Malthus had arrived from Ethiopia two days ahead of schedule and was already unloading at our warehouse, so my services were required far into the night. Jesus departed, the next morning, long before I had risen.

Although I was told by Shemer that the two of them spent many hours together, in the coolness of the atrium, Zacchaeus volunteered little information as to what transpired between them and I never inquired, reasoning that if he wanted me to know he would have told me. Suffice it to say that there was a calm and peaceful tranquillity in his manner, following Jesus' visit, that I had not observed since his youthful years of wedded happiness.

Sad to relate, his serenity was to be short-lived and I was the one who shattered it. I had been at the warehouse early one morning to supervise a large purchase of green figs scheduled for shipment to Damascus, when centurion Marcus Crispus delivered his shocking news to me. I hastened to the palace and found Zacchaeus just finishing his breakfast.

As I entered the dining hall, his smile of welcome quickly faded. "Something is wrong," he announced before I could speak.

I nodded lamely, unable to find the words to tell him.

"Proceed, Joseph," he said. "At least I'll not hear it now on an empty stomach."

I inhaled deeply. "Jesus is dead."

"What?"

"Jesus is dead," I repeated.

"How?" he asked softly.

"Crucified, for sedition against Rome."

"Pontius Pilate?"

"Yes, with assistance from the high priests who claimed Jesus was no more than a false Messiah, a seducer of the people."

Zacchaeus clutched at his chest and closed his eyes. I could see his lips moving. I reached across the table and placed my hand around his neck. Then I heard him say, "Is that all you have to tell me?"

"Is that all? All? Isn't that more than enough?"

His eyes opened, now framed by wrinkles which I recognized were the beginning of a smile. Why was he smiling? He patted my hand, as if to console me, and said, "The tomb where his body was buried—they will find it empty."

"Empty? What are you saying?"

"They will find it empty," he repeated, almost in a whisper.

"How do you know?"

He patted my hand again. "Jesus told me so only two weeks ago, while we were sitting together, outside in the atrium."

CHAPTER 8

Within an hour after I had delivered the news concerning Jesus, Zacchaeus had dispatched a rider to Pontius Pilate, in Jerusalem, bearing his letter of resignation as chief publican. His dictated message, which I transcribed on parchment for his signature, curtly informed the procurator that effective immediately he would no longer serve Rome in any capacity under any conditions.

With that task completed, I prepared to leave the dining hall since my schedule for the day was exceedingly full.

"Not yet, Joseph," he called after me. "There is much more that we must attend to before the sun sets today."

I started to explain that I was already late for my other duties, knowing he would understand, but there was an unusual firmness in his tone that drew me back to my chair.

He sat across from me, occasionally clutching at the tunic covering his chest and wincing. Even his breathing seemed to require great effort.

"Are you ill, Zacchaeus? Is there pain?"

He tried to smile. "My old heart," he said hoarsely, "is only reminding me that it has outlived its years of usefulness—as perhaps I have, also."

"Shall I send Shemer for a physician?"

"No, no, we have too much to do. Now listen to me carefully, Joseph. As you know, I have always maintained that my most valuable assets are the people employed in my stores and stalls and farms. They are all to be notified that, commencing this day, they are no longer working for me but for themselves. Have our clerks draw up the necessary papers immediately, transferring title to each of the farms and stores to those who, through their diligent labor, have contributed so much to each property's success."

I am certain that I made a fool of myself, leaping up as I did and crying out, "You are giving everything away? More than fifty years of your life's work . . . !"

Zacchaeus waited patiently until I was again seated. "I am giving nothing away. Each of those who receive my property must pay a price. A penny is sufficient, I believe," he smiled, "to make the transaction legal. And this palace we shall keep, you and I and Shemer, as our home for the rest of our lives. It is much too large for our simple needs but I am afraid that we are too old and set in our ways to transplant our roots elsewhere."

"Why, Zacchaeus? Why are you doing this?"

"Why not? I have no heirs, nor do you. Why shouldn't we experience that great joy of giving to so many deserving people while we are still alive? And how much land will either of us require when they close our eyes for the final time?"

"But you and I still have many good years. . . ."

"Joseph, one should always retire at one's pinnacle rather than wait until the world begins to look on your efforts with sympathy. Now, there is one more thing. How much money is there in our treasury?"

"H-h-how much? I would estimate at least half a million silver denarii."

"And the value of goods in our warehouse?"

"At least a quarter of a million denarii."

Zacchaeus stroked his chin, eyes half-closed. "The three of us could live well, for twenty years or longer, on fifty thousand denarii, would you not agree, Joseph?"

"Easily, sir."

"And an additional hundred thousand would bear the expenses of the children's party for many years and also see that our city's walls remained clean and white, would you not agree?"

There was little sense in arguing with him. "Yes, sir."

"Very well. Sell all the goods in the warehouse, but only for silver coin. Then, take that revenue plus everything from our treasury, except one hundred and fifty thousand denarii, and see that it is all distributed to the poor of Jericho."

It was all more than I could endure. I buried my face in my hands and tried to collect my composure. "You want me to give six hundred thousand silver denarii—six hundred thousand silver denarii, to the poor?"

"Equally."

"You will make them all wealthy."

"For how long? A week, a month? And why not? Everyone should be wealthy, if only for a day, so that each might realize that being rich is not the ideal condition that most believe it is. And like the land, Joseph, we shall have little need for all that silver when we cease breathing. Let us enjoy the smiling faces of as many children of God as we can, while we are still able to see them."

The following ten days were the busiest of my entire life. Our warehouse was finally emptied of its goods and produce; certificates of ownership were delivered to the new and happy owners of every farm, store, and roadside stall and twenty-three silver coins were distributed to every poor family in the city.

"It is finished," I finally announced to Zacchaeus at dinner one evening. "Except for this house, our empty warehouse, and the money you specified that we put aside, we are bereft of all assets."

"Does it make you feel uncomfortable, Joseph?"

"Not uncomfortable, Master, but sad. I shall miss my work, my worries, my responsibilities, my daily routine. I no longer feel necessary or useful and I dare not think how I can possibly fill my days."

He nodded. "I understand and I share your feelings. How regretful it is that man becomes such a slave to his occupation or his career that he forgets he was created to enjoy this beautiful world and he quickly becomes blind to the miracles of nature that take place before his very eyes, every day. When was the last time you watched a sunset?"

"I cannot even remember."

"Come, let us go up on the roof and enjoy the sun as it disappears behind the brown hills, a luxury that rich men and busy men never have the time to afford."

Afterward we both retired to our chambers but I was unable to sleep. Despite the master's consoling words I was certain that both our lives would become no more than endless days of monotony spent counting the olives on the old tree in the atrium or studying the formations of clouds as they paraded overhead.

How wrong I was. . . .

CHAPTER 9

Early one morning I was roused from an uneasy sleep by Zacchaeus' voice calling my name, again and again. This was such unusual behavior for one who had always bathed and dressed and partaken of breakfast and a stroll, long before I ever crawled from my bed, that his outcries startled me. Still more asleep than awake I hurried, unclothed, across the hall to his chambers.

To my great surprise, the master was sitting upright in his bed. He chuckled as he pointed at my naked condition and said, "Joseph, look at thyself. Art thou becoming more forgetful with your advancing years or is it only concern for my well-being that causes you to ignore a lifetime of shyness?"

I knew not what to say. He reached down to the foot of the bed and handed me his robe. "Wrap this around yourself before the morning chill intrudes itself into your old bones."

I did as I was told, struggling to clear my sleep-filled head as I sat on the edge of his bed.

"Trusted comrade, you and I are survivors. We have endured both failure and success and never allowed either to overwhelm us."

"Yes, Master," I replied, boldly reaching forward

to touch his forehead to assure myself that a burning fever was not the cause of this strange early morning call. His skin was cool to my touch.

"Hear me well, faithful bookkeeper," he continued, ignoring what I had done. "When I awoke, before sunrise, I was unable to move from this bed. I have remained here, until this time, not because my puny legs refused to follow my bidding, but because my mind has been filled with a dream I have just experienced. In it I saw nothing of forms or figures or faces as one usually does in these fanciful flights of slumber. Instead, I could perceive a bright glow, as if it came from a giant star, and I heard a voice thundering, 'Zacchaeus, Zacchaeus—ye have retired from thy obligations too soon. Thy work is not yet completed here on earth! Rise from your bed of self-pity! Go, with your friend Joseph, and attend to those who wait outside thy door!' "

"I do not understand dreams and their symbols, Master. What does it mean?"

Zacchaeus shrugged. "Who can say? Our warehouse is now empty and our stores and farms are in the hands of those who were my most loyal and competent people. Caravans from all points of the compass no longer unload at our docks and merchants who tethered their camels beyond our walls to await my audience already seek assistance elsewhere. More than that, all of my wealth has already been distributed among the poor and I know, full well, that rumors already leap from mouth to mouth, in the city, that the old publican must be close to death. Who then, Joseph, would be foolish enough to stand outside, in our lonely courtyard, and for what purpose?"

"I know not, Zacchaeus."

"And what did that strange voice mean, in my dream, when it said that I have not yet completed my work here on Earth? You, more than anyone, know what I have accomplished. I have fulfilled every goal of my life notwithstanding the loss of my loved ones which was beyond my control. I am at peace—with myself and the world, waiting now only to part with my last possession of value."

"Your last possession . . . ?"

He smiled. "My final breath."

Zacchaeus rose stiffly from his mattress, placed his feet in sandals, and hastily tied their laces. Next, he pulled on a light tunic, stumbled once, and moved toward the door. The cane he had recently taken to using was standing in the corner and I handed it to him but he refused it.

"Come, Joseph, let us see if my dream deals in truth. Let us discover if the hot winds from the desert have deposited anything on our lonely doorstep other than white sand and dried weeds."

At last we stood before the massive bronze door that had been cast from drawings traced by Leah long ago, even before they had moved into the palace.

"Open it, Joseph," he ordered. "Let us not keep a dream in suspense."

I seized the heavy knob. At first it resisted my efforts. Then it turned slowly as the hinges groaned.

I leaned my old body against the ornate floral design and pushed with all my strength.

The door swung open.

We waited, uncertainly, in the doorway, until our eyes became accustomed to the harsh sunlight. "Look!" exclaimed Zacchaeus. "Look!"

I shaded my eyes and followed the direction of his hand. Many years ago, in order to better service the unending parade of caravans to our warehouse, Zacchaeus had hired scores of the city's indigent males, paid them good wages, and constructed a paved road, forty cubits wide, from the city's main thoroughfare directly to the palace and warehouse which lay north of the highway. That road was now choked with people, all marching in our direction and their ranks extended beyond my vision, far back into the city!

"Where can they be going, Master?"

He chuckled. "The road ends here, Joseph."

"But why are they coming? We have already distributed a fortune among them. There is nothing else to give."

Zacchaeus shrugged and moved toward the raised marble balustrade near the wide steps that descended into the courtyard. "Have the years not taught you, my friend, never to worry about the inevitable. Whatever they seek, we shall know soon enough."

Like a giant serpent of many colors, the slow-moving mass curled its way toward us until they were finally near enough for us to hear them. More than anything they sounded to me like a plague of locusts descending on a field of cotton.

"Are you afraid, Joseph?"

"Are you not, sir? Let us go inside, while there is still time, and bolt our door. We shall be safe there."

I turned, hoping that he would follow. Instead, he took hold of my tunic and pulled me gently back to his side. "Joseph, have I never taught you that the secret of confronting any situation in life that threatens to overwhelm and defeat you is to stand fast."

I shook my head in bewilderment. "Never have I had need for such knowledge. During all the years that I served you, whenever an occasion fraught with risk presented itself, I would take that problem to you and you would resolve it."

"To my discredit. Our finest traits and characteristics can grow weak, just as our muscles do, if they are not employed constantly. When I reflect on my past, I realize how derelict I was in so many of my responsibilities to those I supervised, always leading with such a firm rein that much of their self-reliance and initiative was gradually lost. I know I finally succeeded in convincing all of you that this is a world filled with opportunity and that God gives every bird its food, but I fear I failed in not warning you and the others that God will not throw food into your nest."

"I do not understand."

"Joseph, in my old age I have finally come to realize how foolish I have been and how much precious time I wasted feeling sorry for myself, because of this ugly body, instead of being proud and grateful for all that I have managed to accomplish with what I had. Like so many others, I allowed myself to be blinded by envy and self-pity and never gave a thought to counting my blessings.

"I am now convinced," he continued, "that life is just a game, here on Earth, a game where no one need be a loser, no matter what his plight or condition may be. I believe that *everyone* can enjoy the fruits of victory but I am equally as certain that, like all other games, one cannot participate in this mysterious act of living with any hope of satisfaction unless one understands a few simple rules."

"Rules? Rules of life? I know of our Ten Commandments, of course, and I have heard of The Twelve Tables of Roman Law, and also the Code of that Babylonian king, Hammurabi, but never have I heard mention of any rules of life before, even from your lips. By whom were they formulated, and what are they . . . ?"

The crowd had arrived at our gate and was spilling into the courtyard. I shuddered at the sight of them—farmers, shepherds, fishermen, carpenters, people of the street, humanity of all ages—mothers suckling infants cradled closely to their black homespun garments, cripples riding on the backs of sturdy young men clothed only in leather girdles, naked and dirty children scurrying noisily between the legs of their elders, the blind being led or riding in carts, harlots in their gaudy paint, young couples looking hungry and forlorn, holding hands. It was as if all the poor, the unfortunate, and the misfits of Jericho had joined together to seek collective refuge on our doorstep.

"Hail to our benefactor, hail to our benefactor!" they shouted.

"Do you hear them?" I screamed in the master's ear. "They are seeking more alms! Tell them there is no more to give and send them away!"

"I cannot do that, Joseph. They are all my brothers and sisters. They are all your brothers and sisters, too."

"I have no brothers and sisters," I cried out. "Send them back to their misery before they overrun us and take away what little we have. They are an army—at least ten thousand strong—and we are only two old men."

Zacchaeus ignored me and raised both hands, palms extended toward the crowd. Suddenly there was silence, even among the children.

"What is it that ye seek of me?"

From our vantage point on the landing, several cubits above the courtyard, we watched as thousands of heads turned from side to side in nervous consternation. No one, it seemed, had the courage to reply.

Zacchaeus waited patiently. Then he asked, "Why have ye come here, this day?"

Again there was silence, for I cannot remember how long, before the mob gradually parted and we could discern an approaching figure, white of hair and beard, dressed in a dark blue robe and carrying a large staff for support.

Zacchaeus recognized him first. "It is Ben-hadad!"

Ben-hadad was, without question, the city's most beloved patriarch. For as long as I can remember, even back to those days when our business was struggling merely to survive, he could always be found, from sunrise to sunset, in the shaded doorway of the bazaar where his son displayed and sold rich and colorful bolts of the fabric known as damask. Through the years Ben-hadad had become as much a landmark as the city's aqueducts and gates, squatting on his carpet, day after day with eyes half-closed, observing the world and the seasons pass before him. On many occasions in the distant past, he had been selected by the people to intercede in their behalf with the Roman legate in Antioch, especially whenever the mercenaries of Rome abused the local merchants. He had always succeeded in his missions.

Two young men rushed forward to offer their assistance to the venerable old man as he began his obviously painful climb up the smooth marble steps. He spoke briefly to them, in words I could not hear, and they quickly returned to their place in the crowd.

Slowly he ascended toward us, accompanied by the tapping sound of his staff on the stone as he placed it on each step to brace himself. The throng remained still, watching and waiting.

CHAPTER 10

❧❦

"Greetings!" said Ben-hadad, raising his staff to both of us.

"Welcome to our home, sir!" replied Zacchaeus. "Long ago I had abandoned all hope of ever having you accept my countless invitations to dine with us here. And now you appear, old friend, when I have little to offer and you bring with you more guests than I can accommodate."

Ben-hadad smiled and wiped his thin fingers across his moist brow. "We did not come for food, sir. At least not the kind that one ingests through the mouth."

I tried to whisper, "I told you so. They are after something!"

The crowd moved closer to the steps, straining to hear, pressing so tightly against one another that not a single stone of the courtyard was visible.

"It is a great pleasure and honor to have you here at last, Ben-hadad, no matter what your reason is for coming."

The two embraced. Then Ben-hadad stepped back and spoke slowly in a loud voice, for the benefit of the throng. "Zacchaeus, your name and your success are known throughout the land and even from sea to sea. But we, the citizens of Jericho, hold you in the highest esteem, not because of your world-wide fame but for the helping hand you have extended to all of us, for so many years. Charity is, indeed, true love in action and we have been fortunate enough to bask in the warmth of your love for half a century."

I moved closer to the master but could not find the courage to give him a warning nudge. Benhadad continued, "To die and leave behind one's wealth for distribution is the very essence of selfishness indulged in usually by those of means who gave not even a penny when alive. This has obviously never been your plan, Zacchaeus, as witnessed by your countless contributions to the needy and the helpless. Nor have you shared only your gold and silver but also yourself. It is always difficult to be charitable with wisdom. To give alms is nothing unless one gives thought also for it is written, 'not blessed is he that feedeth the poor but blessed is he that considereth the poor.' A little consideration and a handful of kindness are often worth far more than gold."

Zacchaeus bowed his head, unable as always to deal with such praise. "We are rich only through what we give—and we are poor only through what we keep."

"Then you are, in truth, the richest of men."

"Ye make too much of my meager efforts," protested Zacchaeus. "There are many here, today, who have given more. Every kind act is an act of charity. But please tell me, sir, before my curiosity overwhelms me, what is it that brings you and so much of the city's population to my door?"

Ben-hadad turned and swept his staff across the vast throng, waiting until he had silence. "Zacchaeus, it has been said that if you would plant for days, plant flowers. If you would plant for years, plant trees. If you would plant for eternity, plant ideas. These people are here, this day, to beg of you to implant in them the secrets of success that enabled you to reach the top of the mountain in a single lifetime.

"We are all familiar with the story of your career," he continued. "We know that your mother and father were both lost to you, at an early age, and how it became your sad lot to labor long in the fields while other children attended school. In order to instill hope and ambition in their young, parents now tell them, by the light of their fires at night, how you were able to overcome all those handicaps and more, including the afflictions of your body, to become the greatest success in the world. But—there is information that they are unable to pass on to their offspring—because they do not know!"

I held my breath. I am certain that Zacchaeus did, also.

Ben-hadad pounded the tip of his staff against the marble floor, again and again. "What they cannot tell their children, sir, is *how* you managed to accomplish so much! You—an orphan with no education, as poor as one can be—and deformed, please forgive me, so that others mocked you. If ever an individual was doomed to a life of misery and poverty as a beggar of alms it was you. How, Zaccheus, were you able to make so much of your life when others, blessed by God with good health and schooling and sage counsel from their elders, are failures? How is it that so many, with far greater potential for success and wealth than you, live each day not knowing whence the crumbs of their next meal will come? Are there special principles that ye have followed in your numerous profitable undertakings? Are there secrets of achievement known only to a few? Are there unique guidelines or hidden paths that one can follow to a better life that are unknown to the masses who struggle so hard, each day, merely to survive?"

"There *are* rules," I heard Zaccheus whisper, half to himself.

Ben-hadad cocked his head. "What did you say, sir?"

"Rules," Zaccheus repeated. "Rules for living." He spoke haltingly as if the words had difficulty in forming in his throat.

"I do not understand."

"I was telling Joseph, only today, that I have reached the conclusion that life is only a game— but like all other games it has certain rules that must be observed and applied in order to enjoy the playing. Furthermore, if we follow its rules our chances for victory are greatly multiplied. However, sad to say, most of the people are so busy merely struggling to survive that they never even have the opportunity to learn the few simple commandments necessary for success—a success, by the way, which has little to do with fame or gold."

The older man stepped closer to his host. "I consider myself an educated man, Zacchaeus, yet in all my years I have never heard of such commandments. Where are they written down so that we all might benefit from them?"

"They are not written down, Ben-hadad."

"But you know them?"

"Most of them, I believe, all learned the hard way."

"This young prophet, Jesus, whom they are now claiming has risen from the dead—did he teach you any of these commandments when he visited with you before his arrest and execution?"

Zacchaeus smiled. "No, they were known to me long before then. But after our long talk together I do not believe that he would disagree with any of them."

Ben-hadad stared intently at my master. "I am certain that you did not intend to carry such an invaluable treasure to your grave, Zacchaeus. You have shared so much of yourself with us for so long, will ye not share your commandments of success also? Is not everyone entitled to the opportunity to change their lives for the better?"

Zacchaeus closed his eyes and stood motionless. The crowd began to murmur among themselves until he finally opened his eyes and nodded.

When the cheering finally subsided he said, "It will take time for me to organize my thoughts before I transcribe them to parchment, with Joseph's help, but I shall do it."

Ben-hadad, to my surprise, shook his head. "No, no, a single parchment copy of your commandments of success will not suffice. Look out there at the thousands who need help and guidance. Should not each of them have access to your words so that they can be absorbed into every heart and mind and soul in due time?"

"To make copies for everyone in the city would take years upon years," I interrupted, unable to control myself any longer. "You are suggesting the impossible, Ben-hadad!"

Zacchaeus placed his hand on my shoulder and pulled me toward him. "Remember, Joseph, long ago I told you that nothing is impossible unless one agrees that it is?"

"But, Master," I protested, "how can you spread your words among such a multitude so that they all will benefit? That, indeed, is an impossibility, even for you!"

Zacchaeus rubbed my shoulder consolingly and pointed to the distant walls of the city, sparkling in their whiteness beneath the bright morning sun.

"Beginning this very afternoon, I shall dictate to you what I believe should be included in The Commandments of Success. Although they are all very simple truths it will still be a long and painful process for me since I am better with my hands, as you know, than with words. Still, with your help we shall prevail. When they are finally corrected and completed, to my satisfaction, we shall have their words painted in large red letters on the inside panels of the city's clean white walls, near the west gate, so that the greatest possible number may view them every day, if they wish. And that will be my final gift to them, my bequest to all who cry out for help, my small legacy to the world which has given me so much more than I deserve."

"It will be a monumental undertaking," I gasped.

"But worth it," he said, "if we only touch one life."

And so it came to pass that within fifty days of his promise, the words of Zacchaeus were displayed on the west wall of Jericho, in the tongue of the common man, Aramaic, and large crowds came each day, even caravans from afar, to read with their own eyes and to learn how it was possible to transform their days of hopeless drudgery into a lifetime of fulfillment and peace.

When I teasingly inquired of Zacchaeus why he had written only nine commandments his answer was brief. "Because God gave us Ten Commandments and it is not worth the slightest risk of tempting anyone to be foolish enough to make any comparisons between the two.

"Obeying the ten Laws of God," he added, "will provide us with admission to heaven. Obeying the nine Commandments of Success may give anyone a taste of that heaven, here on earth."

CHAPTER 11

The First Commandment of Success

Thou Must Labor Each Day As If Thy Life Hung In The Balance.

You were not created for a life of idleness. You cannot eat from sunrise to sunset or drink or play or make love. Work is not your enemy but your friend. If all manners of labor were forbidden to thee you would fall to your knees and beg an early death.

You need not love the tasks you do. Even kings dream of other occupations. Yet you must work and it is how you do, not what you do, that determines the course of your life. No man who is careless with his hammer will ever build a palace.

You may work grudgingly or you may work gratefully; you may work as a human or you may work as an animal. Still, there is no work so rude that you may not exalt it; no work so demeaning that you cannot breathe a soul into it; no work so dull that you may not enliven it.

Always perform all that is asked of you and more. Thy reward will come.

Know that there is only one certain method of

attaining success and that is through hard work. If you are unwilling to pay this price for distinction, be prepared for a lifetime of mediocrity and poverty.

Pity those who abuse you and ask why you deliver so much in return for so little. Those who give less, receive less.

Never be tempted to diminish your efforts, even if ye should labor for another. You are no less a success if someone else is paying you to work for yourself. Always do your best. What you plant now, you will harvest later.

Be grateful for your tasks and their demands. If it were not for your work, no matter how distasteful it may seem, you could neither eat so much, nor relish so pleasantly, nor sleep so soundly, nor be so healthful, nor enjoy the secure smiles of gratitude from those who love you for what you are, not for what you do.

CHAPTER 12

The Second Commandment of Success

Thou Must Learn That With Patience Ye Can Control Thy Destiny.

Know that the more enduring thy patience, the more certain thy reward. There is no great accomplishment that is not the result of patient working and waiting.

Life is not a race. No road will be too long for you if you advance deliberately and without haste. Avoid, like the plague, every carriage that halts to offer you a swift journey to wealth, fame, and power. Life has such hard conditions, even at its best, that the temptations when they appear, can destroy you. Walk. You are able.

Patience is bitter, but it: fruit is sweet. With patience you can bear up under any adversity and survive any defeat. With patience you can control your destiny and have what you will.

Patience is the key to contentment, for you and for those who must live with you.

Realize that you cannot hurry success any more than the lilies of the field can bloom before their season. What pyramid was ever built but by a stone at a time? How poor are they who have not patience. What wound did ever heal but by degrees?

Every priceless attribute which wise men trumpet as necessary for the achievement of success is useless without patience. To be brave without patience can kill you. To be ambitious without patience can destroy the most promising of careers. To strive for wealth without patience will only separate you from your thin purse. And to persevere without patience is always impossible. Who can hold on, who can persevere, without the waiting that attends it?

Patience is power. Employ it to stiffen your spirit, sweeten your temper, stifle your anger, bury your envy, subdue your pride, bridle your tongue, restrain your hand, and deliver you whole, in due time, to the life you deserve.

CHAPTER 13

The Third Commandment of Success

Thou Must Chart Thy Course With Care Or Ye Will Drift Forever.

Without hard work you have learned that you will never succeed. So also, without patience. Yet one may work diligently and be more patient than Job and still never rise above mediocrity unless plans are drawn and goals established.

No ship ever lifted anchor and set sail without a destination. No army ever marched off to battle without a plan for victory. No olive tree ever displayed its flowers without promise of the fruit to come.

It is impossible to advance properly in life without goals.

Life is a game with few players and many spectators. Those who watch are the hordes who wander through life with no dreams, no goals, no plans even for tomorrow. Do not pity them. They made their choice when they made no choice. To watch the races from the stands is safe. Who can stumble, who can fall, who can be jeered if they make no effort to participate?

Art thou a player? As a player ye cannot lose. Those who win may carry off the fruits of victory and yet those who are defeated, today, have learned valuable lessons that may turn the tide for them tomorrow.

What do you want of your life? Consider long and well before you decide, for you may attain what you seek. Is it wealth, power, a loving home, peace of mind, land, respect, position? Whatever your goals may be, fix them in your mind and never let loose. Understand that even this may not be sufficient, for life is unfair. Not all who work hard and patiently and have goals will achieve success. Without any of these three ingredients, however, failure is a certainty.

Give yourself every chance to succeed. And if you fail, fail trying!

Draw up your plans today. Ask yourself where you will be, a year from today, if you are still doing the things you are doing now. Then decide where you would prefer to be in terms of wealth or position or whatever your dreams may be. Next, plan what you must do, in the next twelve months, to reach your goal.

And finally, do it!

CHAPTER 14

The Fourth Commandment of Success

Thou Must Prepare For Darkness While Traveling In The Sunlight.

Realize that no condition is permanent. There are seasons in your life just as in nature. No situation which confronts thee, good or bad, will last.

Make no plans that extend beyond a year. In life, as in war, plans of long-range have no significance. All depends on the way unexpected movements of the enemy, that cannot be foreseen, are met, and how the whole matter is handled.

Your enemy, if you are not prepared, can be the cycles of life, mysterious rhythms of ups and downs like the great seas that rise and fall on the shores of the world. High tide and low, sunrise and sunset, wealth and poverty, joy and despair—each of these forces will prevail in their time.

Pity the rich man, riding the high tide of what seems an endless chain of great accomplishments. When calamity strikes he is ill-prepared and comes to utter ruin. Always be prepared for the worst.

Pity the poor man, buried in the low tide of failure

after failure, sadness after sadness. Eventually he ceases trying, just as the tide is changing and success is reaching out to embrace him. Never stop trying.

Always have faith that conditions will change. Though your heart be heavy and your body bruised and your purse empty and there is no one to comfort you—hold on. Just as you know the sun will rise, so also believe that your period of misfortune must end. It was always so. It will always be.

And if your work and your patience and your plans have brought you good fortune, seek out those whose tide is low and lift them up. Prepare for your future. The day may come when what thou hast done for another will also be done for thee.

Remember that nothing is constant, but treasure the love you receive above all. It will survive long after your gold and good health have vanished.

And plan to lose even that love, after a time, knowing that one day you will be reunited for all eternity in a place where there are no cycles, no ups and downs, no pain or sorrow, and above all, no failures.

CHAPTER 15

❦

The Fifth Commandment of Success

Thou Must Smile In The Face Of Adversity Until It Surrenders.

You are wiser than most, once you realize that adversity is never the permanent condition of man. And yet this wisdom alone is not sufficient. Adversity and failure can destroy you while you wait patiently for your fortune to change. Deal with them in only one way.

Welcome them both, with open arms!

Since this injunction goes against all logic or reason, it is the most difficult to understand or master.

Let the tears you shed, over your misfortunes, cleanse thine eyes so that ye might see the truth. Realize that he who wrestles with you always strengthens your nerves and sharpens your skills. Your antagonist is always, in the end, your best helper.

Adversity is the rain in your life, cold, comfortless, and unfriendly. Yet from that season are born the lily, the rose, the date, and the pomegranate. Who can tell what great things you will bring forth after you have been parched by the heat of tribulation and drenched by the rains of affliction? Even the desert blooms after a storm.

Adversity is also your greatest teacher. You will learn little from your victories but when you are pushed, tormented, and defeated you will acquire great knowledge, for only then will you become acquainted with your true self since you are free, at last, from those who flatter thee. And who are your friends? When adversity engulfs you is the best time to count them.

Remind thyself, in the darkest moments, that every failure is only a step toward success, every detection of what is false directs you toward what is true, every trial exhausts some tempting form of error, and every adversity will only hide, for a time, your path to peace and fulfillment.

CHAPTER 16

The Sixth Commandment of Success

Thou Must Realize That Plans Are Only Dreams Without Action.

He whose ambition creeps instead of soars, who is always uncertain, who procrastinates instead of acts, struggles in vain against failure.

Is he not imprudent who, seeing the tide making toward him, will sleep until the sea overwhelms him? Is he not foolish who, given the opportunity to improve his lot, will deliberate until his neighbor is chosen instead?

Only action gives to life its strength, its joy, its purpose. The world will always determine your worth by the deeds you do. Who can measure your talents by the thoughts you have or the emotions you feel? And how will you proclaim your abilities if you are always a spectator and never a player?

Take heart. Know that activity and sadness are eternal opposites. When thy muscles are straining and fingers are gripping and feet are moving and your mind is occupied with the task at hand you have little time for self-pity and remorse. Action is the balm that will heal any wound.

Remember that patience is the art of waiting, with faith, for the life you deserve through your good works, but action is the power that makes good works possible. Even the length of thy wait, for the good things you have earned, seems less when you are busy.

No one will act for you. Your plans will remain no more than an idler's dream until you rise up and fight against the forces that would keep ye small. To take action is always dangerous, but to sit and wait for the good things of life to fall into thy lap is the only calling where failures excel.

Everything that lies between your cradle and your grave is always marked with uncertainty. Laugh at your doubts and move ahead. And if it is leisure you seek, instead of work, take heart. The more you do, the more you can do, and the busier you are, the more leisure you will have.

Act or ye will be acted upon.

CHAPTER 17

❦❦❦

The Seventh Commandment of Success

Thou Must Sweep Cobwebs From Thy Mind Before They Imprison Thee.

The mind is its own place, and in itself can make a heaven of hell, or a hell of heaven.

Why do you still think of the love that your own foolishness and temerity caused you to lose, long ago? Will that memory help your digestion this morning?

Why do you still grieve over your failures? Will tears improve thy skills while you labor for your family, today?

Why do you still remember the face of he who harmed thee? Will the thought of sweet revenge enable you to sleep better tonight?

Friends dead, jobs failed, words that wounded, grudges undeserved, money lost, sorrows unhealed, goals failed, ambitions destroyed, loyalties betrayed—why have ye preserved all this evil clutter as if it had value? Why have ye allowed such cobwebs of infamy to gather in the attic of your mind until there is scarcely room for a happy thought about this day?

Sweep out the tragic strands to the past that have accumulated with the years. Their festering entrails will choke you, in time, if you are not diligent. The ability to forget is a virtue, not a vice.

And yet, to know that yesterday with all its mistakes and cares, its pain and tears, has passed forever and cannot harm you, is not enough. So also must you believe that you can do nothing about tomorrow, with its possible heartaches and blunders, until the sun rises again. All you have, that you can fashion as you wish, is the hour at hand.

Never let worry about tomorrow cast a shadow over today. What madness it is to be expecting evil before it comes. Waste not a moment's thought on that which may never happen. Concern thyself only with the present. He who worries about calamities suffers them twice over.

Forget what is past and let God concern himself with the future. He is far more capable than you.

CHAPTER 18

The Eighth Commandment of Success

Thou Must Lighten Thy Load If Ye Would Reach Thy Destination.

How different you are now from the infant that you were. You came into this world with nothing, but through the years you have allowed yourself to be weighed down by so much heavy baggage, in the name of security, that your journey through life has become a punishment instead of a pleasure.

Lighten thy load, beginning today.

Understand that the true worth of man is measured by the objects he refuses to pursue or acquire. The great blessings of life are already within you, or within your reach. Open thine eyes to the truth before you stumble past the very treasures you seek. Love, peace of mind, and happiness are jewels which no condition of fortune, no amount of land or coin, can either exalt or depress.

What reward is there in gold and silks and palaces if their possession destroys the happiness you have so blindly taken for granted? The greatest falsehood in the world is that money and property can fill your life with joy. If wealth becomes part of your baggage you become poor, for then you will be no more than an ass whose back bows under the weight of gold you must carry until death unloads thy cargo.

Of all the needless materials that you embrace, of all the pleasures you enjoy, you will still carry no more out of this world than out of a dream. Admit riches grudgingly into thy home, but never into thy heart.

And envy no man his grand possessions. His baggage would be too heavy for you, as it is for him. You could not sacrifice, as he does, health, peace, honor, love, quiet, and conscience, to obtain them. The price is so high that the bargain becomes, in the end, a great loss.

Simplify your life. He is richest who is content with the least.

CHAPTER 19

The Ninth Commandment of Success

Thou Must Never Forget That It Is Always Later Than Ye Think.

Remember that the black camel of death is always near. Abide always with the thought that you will not live forever. Such is the irony of life that this knowledge, alone, will enable you to taste the sweetness of each new day instead of bemoaning the darkness of your nights.

All of us have been dying, hour by hour, since the moment we were born. Realizing this, let all things be placed in their proper perspective so that thine eyes will be opened until you see that those mountains which threaten you are only anthills and those beasts which seek to devour you are only gnats.

Live with death as your companion but never fear it. Many are so afraid to die that they never live. Have compassion for them. How can they know that the happiness of death is concealed from us so that we might better endure life?

Imagine that you are called away forever, tonight. Shed tears now, while you are able, for that day of play you promised your family last week, and the week before, a day of love and laughter you were always too busy pursuing gold to enjoy. And now they have your gold, it is true, but with all of it they cannot buy even a fleeting moment of your smile.

Shed tears now, while your heart still beats, for the flowers you will never smell, the good deeds you will never do, the mother you will never visit, the music you will never hear, the pains you will never comfort, the tasks you will never complete, the dreams you will never realize.

Remember that it is always later than you think. Fasten this warning deep in your mind, not for sorrow's sake but to remind yourself that today may be all you have.

Learn to live with death but never flee from it.

For if you die, you will be with God. And if you live, He will be with you.

CHAPTER 20

"I don't know," sighed Zacchaeus, nodding toward the lines of neatly red-lettered words with each commandment separated from the next by a cubit or more of white wall. "The truth is there, for all to see, but do they understand that merely reading the words will have no effect on their lives unless they decide to act on them?"

"Act, or ye will be acted upon?" I said, pointing toward the last line of the commandment on the sixth panel.

He nodded. The two of us were sitting in our favorite open carriage, our progress momentarily halted near the west gate by the immense crowd that was gathered near the wall just as it had every day for the past month.

"Listen to that strange sound they are making," he said.

"They are reading the commandments aloud," I explained. "When one has finished with the first, he or she moves on to the second, and then the third. . . ."

I motioned with the reins toward a well-dressed young man standing close to the wall. "Look at him, Master. He is copying your words on parchment. And there is another, and another, all doing the same."

"That is well and good," Zacchaeus replied, "but those scholars should be told that words on paper are as powerless as words on stone unless they are translated into deeds."

We watched the ebb and flow of the masses, from all walks of life, for several moments before the master shook his head and pointed to a group of six older men arguing loudly near the wall. "They are very simple rules, as I have written them, but perhaps they are still not clear. All laws and rules should be like clothes. They should be made to fit the people they are meant to serve. I have this urge to stand beneath each panel, as a teacher might, and explain the essence of each commandment."

"Perhaps you underestimate their intelligence."

"No, never. What concerns me is their spirit. Most of them have had to live with adversity for so long that I fear they have lost all ambition to improve their lives. People retain their strength long after they have lost their will, but what good are your muscles if your desire has vanished? I fear they will read what I have written, because of the novelty of its presentation there on the wall, but return immediately to their old ways of living and thinking, through habit if nothing else."

"Zacchaeus, if that were true I would not see the same faces here every day when I pass by. These people are not merely reading your words, they are memorizing them!"

"Good, good. If only . . ."

"What is wrong, sir?"

"Look, Joseph!" he said in a whisper, pointing over my shoulder to a troop of Roman cavalry, at least thirty strong, riding two abreast in our direction. At its head, on a gray horse, rode a familiar figure wearing helmet and breastplate as if he were prepared for battle.

"Pilate!"

Zacchaeus winced. "And his men have their swords drawn as if they were expecting trouble. What do you suppose has brought the procurator from Jerusalem this time?"

We were not long in finding out. Behind the cavalry rolled three long-bodied wagons, each drawn by six horses and piled high with ladders. Riding atop the ladders in each wagon were at least a dozen soldiers.

The crowd grudgingly moved back in silence as the three wagons halted near the wall and the soldiers leaped to the ground, swiftly unloading the ladders and leaning them against the wall. As they worked, their fellow-legionaries who were still on horseback turned their mounts to face the throng.

Zacchaeus squeezed my arm and pointed toward the third wagon where soldiers were now pouring white liquid from a large copper tank into pails.

"They are going to whitewash our wall, Joseph."

"But our wall does not need whitewashing."

"That one apparently does," he said sadly, sweeping his hand in the direction of the panels that displayed The Commandments of Success.

When those in the forefront of the crowd finally realized what the soldiers were preparing to do they surged forward shouting, "No, no, no!" until the cavalrymen raised their swords above their heads menacingly.

"There will be bloodshed, Joseph, unless we put a stop to this," Zacchaeus muttered, climbing down from the carriage with difficulty. Trembling, I followed as he made his way through the mob who cheered when they recognized him. When Pilate turned and saw us approaching he dismounted and removed his helmet. With hands on hips and feet wide apart the procurator shook his fist in our direction and shouted, "Little old man, you have gone too far with your wall painting, this time!"

"Why?" Zacchaeus asked calmly. "What has been done that is so terrible?"

Now Pilate shook his fist at the red-lettered wall. "The laws of Rome are sufficient for this ... this rabble!"

"But those are not laws that you see on the wall. They are merely rules, simple rules that one might follow for a better and happier life. Many of them are similar to the writings of some of the greatest minds in Rome and Athens. Why do you condemn here what many respect in your own country?"

Pilate stepped closer and cleared his throat. His spittle landed on my master's cheek but Zacchaeus never flinched. "I should have you executed," the procurator roared, "for treason against the empire, you disloyal publican, you sorry excuse for a man!"

"Why?"

"You know why."

"For the same reason that you crucified Jesus?"

Pilate paled. "You are an agitator, just as he was. You incite the people with false promises of a kind of life they will never know. Look at them! Ignorant, dirty, diseased, penniless! Who gave you a license to prescribe for them? And what will you tell them if your medicine fails to cure them? What will you suggest next, if your magic rules do not work? Revolt, perhaps? Will you inform them that Rome, after all, is the true root of their problems and that Caesar is to blame for the crusts of bread they must eat? You are a dangerous man, Zacchaeus. You seduce the people with sweet temptations and in their condition they will follow anyone foolish enough to lead them. You . . . and that Jesus!"

Zacchaeus smiled. "Blessed are the poor in spirit for they . . ."

"Enough!" Pilate cried, turning toward the soldiers who were waiting at the foot of the ladders, pail and swab in hand. He raised his arm and they commenced their climb up the wall.

Suddenly, and accompanied by loud shouts, a youth raced from out of the crowd and began pulling at the low rungs of one of the ladders which held an ascending soldier. Two legionaries immediately leaped from their horses and while one of them held the young man's arms, from behind, the other thrust his sword deep into his stomach. Then he waved his blood-covered blade at the moaning crowd as if daring anyone else to come forward.

Zacchaeus limped from my side directly to the fallen youth, ignoring the two soldiers and their poised blades. He knelt down and gently cradled the boy's head in his arms. It had been a long time since I had seen my master cry.

By nightfall The Commandments of Success had been completely obliterated and the wall near the west gate was white again and Pilate had returned, with his men, to Jerusalem.

CHAPTER 21

Ever since Zacchaeus had relinquished his responsibilities, transferred ownership of his farms and stalls, and distributed his fortune to the poor, our living habits had changed. Now it was he who slept until long after sunrise and it was I who, after fitful nights, would rise early and walk through the streets of Jericho for want of something better to do.

On the morning after Pilate's terrible act, for reasons I shall never understand, my feet had taken me along the cobbled road inside the wall until I eventually arrived near the west gate just as the sun was rising above the distant mountains. Because of the early hour I was alone in the street. I shall never forget that dawn.

There, on the gleaming white wall of fresh paint, with every word lettered in red exactly as they had been until yesterday morning, were The Commandments of Success!

I remember falling to my knees, bewildered and shocked. I rubbed my eyes until they hurt, thinking that they must be playing tricks on me in the early changing light. Was I having delusions? Had the tragedy of yesterday affected my mind? I heard a cough and jumped. Approaching was a figure in blue, his head bowed deep in prayer.

"Ben-hadad," I cried, "is it you?"

The old man slowed his step. "Joseph? What are you doing by the side of the road at this time of morning? Are you hurt? Have bandits attacked you and robbed your purse?"

"Ben-hadad, look!" I cried, pointing to the wall. "Tell me that my eyes do not deceive me. What do you see?"

His actions were all the confirmation I needed. Tears began streaming down his wrinkled face as he slowly slumped to his knees near me. "It is a miracle, Joseph, a miracle! To think that I should live to see such a day! Twice, now, God has used the walls of Jericho to assure us that He has not turned his back on man's search for a better life. And look there, Joseph, look there!" he gasped, pointing beyond the panel which displayed The Ninth Commandment of Success. "Something has been added to the words of our friend, Zacchaeus!"

"It cannot be," I cried, rubbing my eyes again. "It cannot be!"

"Did your master have a tenth commandment which he chose not to present?"

"I do not know, for a certainty. He did mention, one day as we worked, that there were twenty or thirty rules and all were important but he believed that nine would be sufficient to play the game of life with a good chance of being victorious. And the number ten, he said, was reserved for God's Commandments."

"But now we do have ten," Ben-hadad said breathlessly.

"Yes, and the tenth is lettered in red, in the same size and style as the other nine! I must hurry. I must run and tell Zacchaeus . . . !"

"Wait," the old man said, clutching my sleeve. "Before you go, let us read The Tenth Commandment of Success together, you and I. After all, it is not every day that one can share a miracle."

And so, holding hands, we read the words. . . .

CHAPTER 22

The Tenth Commandment of Success

Thou Must Never Strive To Be Anything But Thyself.

To be what you are and to become what you are capable of becoming is the secret of a happy life.

Every living soul has different talents, different desires, different faculties. Be yourself. Try to be anything else but your genuine self, even if you deceive the entire world, and you will be ten thousand times worse than nothing.

Never waste any effort into elevating yourself into something you are not, to please another. Never put on false masks to gratify your vanity. Never strain to be valued for your accomplishments or you will cease to be valued for thyself.

Consider the plants and the animals of the field, how they live. Does a cotton plant bear even one apple? Does a pomegranate tree ever produce an orange? Does a lion attempt to fly?

Only man, of all living things, foolishly strives to be other than what he was intended to be until life marks him a misfit. Misfits are the failures of the world, always chasing after a more fruitful career they will never find unless they look behind them.

You cannot choose your calling. Your calling chooses you. You have been blessed with special skills that are yours alone. Use them, whatever they may be, and forget about wearing another's hat. A talented chariot driver can win gold and renown with his skills. Let him pick figs and he would starve.

No one can take your place. Realize this and be yourself. You have no obligation to succeed. You have only the obligation to be true to yourself.

Do the very best that you can, in the things you do best, and you will know, in thy soul, that you are the greatest success in the world.

CHAPTER 23

❦❦

My old heart was pounding furiously and my legs were nearly numb by the time I arrived back at the palace. Had not a startled Shemer caught me as soon as I opened the front door I am certain that I would have collapsed on the tiles.

He tried to lead me to a nearby bench, in the foyer, but I would have none of it. After drawing several deep breaths I finally managed to ask, "Where is the master? Is he still asleep?"

"No, sire. He arose early and has already eaten. Are you hungry?"

I shook my head. "And where is he now?"

Shemer gestured toward the rear of the palace. "He said that he was going to walk in the garden. You will probably find him near Leah's tomb. Lately, he has been spending much time there."

My legs now felt as if they had been attacked by a horde of hornets and sharp pains were stabbing at my back and chest but I managed to stagger down the long hallway and out the back door that led to the garden. The tomb was more than a hundred cubits away, shaded by four olive trees, but I saw him immediately, sitting on the raised edge that surrounded the marble structure and leaning back against its side wall.

Even at that distance I could not remain silent. Limping toward him as swiftly as I could, I shouted, "Zacchaeus, Zacchaeus, I bring you great tidings! A miracle has happened! A miracle! You will not believe it until you see for yourself!"

The pains in my chest multiplied in ferocity with every step. "Zacchaeus—Master—you must come. Hurry! Your words. . . . The Commandments of Success . . . the wall. . . ."

His eyes were closed. I knelt beside him and took his clasped hands in mine to shake him gently awake and then I knew that I never would. I leaned forward and placed my cheek against his cold fingers and they immediately parted, releasing a small white object that fell to the stone and shattered.

I reached down among the fragments and picked up a tiny bird, delicately carved out of ivory—all that now remained intact of a baby's rattle that I had seen only once, so very long ago. I kissed it and finally began to weep, not tears of grief but joy.

That little bird was finally free of its earthly cage—and so was my beloved master.

ABOUT THE AUTHOR

OG MANDINO is the most widely read inspirational and self-help author in the world today. His fourteen books have sold more than twenty-five million copies in eighteen languages. Thousands of people from all walks of life have openly credited Og Mandino with turning their lives around and for the miracle they have found in his words. His books of wisdom, inspiration, and love include *A Better Way to Live; The Choice; The Christ Commission; The Gift of Acabar; The Greatest Miracle in the World; The Greatest Salesman in the World; The Greatest Salesman in the World, Part II: The End of the Story; The Greatest Secret in the World; The Greatest Success in the World; Mission: Success!; Og Mandino's University of Success; and The Return of the Ragpicker*.

"May the Lord
touch your heart
with his finger of love
and leave a fingerprint
no one can rub off."

—ROBERT H. SCHULLER,
from *Be Happy You Are Loved*

WORDS OF INSPIRATION FROM ROBERT H. SCHULLER

____26458-3	The Be (Happy) Attitudes	$5.99/$7.99 Canada
____28867-9	Believe in the God Who Believes in You	$5.99/$7.99
____28182-8	Success is Never Ending, Failure is Never Final	$5.99/$7.99
____27332-9	Tough Times Never Last, but Tough People Do!	$5.99/$7.50
____24704-2	Tough-Minded Faith for Tender-Hearted People	$5.99/$7.99
____56167-7	Life's Not Fair, but God Is Good	$5.50/$6.99